British Cross-Channel Railway Passenger Ships

The 1,445-ton Brittany *was built in 1933 for the Southern Railway's Jersey–St Malo route: her 39-year career took her to more than 60 different ports.*

British Cross-Channel Railway Passenger Ships

John de S. Winser

PSL

AN IMPRINT OF HAYNES PUBLISHING

Patrick Stephens Limited

The 1948 steamer St Patrick *at St Peter Port, Guernsey, in September 1950.*

First published in 1994

A catalogue record for this book is available from the British Library.

ISBN 1 85260 459 X

Patrick Stephens Limited
is an imprint of Haynes Publishing,
Sparkford, near Yeovil, Somerset, BA22 7JJ

Printed in Great Britain by Butler & Tanner Ltd, Frome and London

Typeset by MS Filmsetting Limited, Frome, Somerset

Front endpaper: *Jersey's Elizabeth Castle and St Aubins Bay make a splendid background to this May 1959 view of St Helier Harbour, showing* Falaise *in port during a cruise call.*

Title pages: *The scene in Dieppe Harbour on 15th August 1937, with (left to right)* Brighton, *just arrived from Newhaven; the French cross-Channel vessel* Rouen *at the quay and, alongside her, the 1913 Southern Railway steamer* Paris *on a day excursion from Brighton.*

Rear endpaper: *The 1949 Strait of Dover steamer* Maid of Orleans.

Patrick Stephens Limited, is an imprint of Haynes Publishing, and, has published authoritative, quality books for enthusiasts for more than a quarter of a century. During that time the company has established a reputation as one of the world's leading publishers of books on aviation, maritime, military, model-making, motor cycling, motoring, motor racing, railway and railway modelling subjects. Readers or authors with suggestions for books they would like to see published are invited to write to: The Editorial Director, Patrick Stephens Limited, Sparkford, Nr. Yeovil, Somerset, BA22 7JJ.

Contents

Note: the years of introduction into civilian service are given when the same name has been used for more than one ship featured.

A tranquil scene outside Dover Harbour in June 1971, as the 31-year-old Invicta *heads for Calais.*

Introduction

When the railway-owned Sealink steamer *Caesarea* made her final crossing of the Strait of Dover in October 1980, it was an historical event. She was the last of a long and impressive line of British cross-Channel railway passenger ships, a type made extinct by the ultimate dominance of the car ferry vessel.

This book is intended to put into focus the major ships which were expressly designed for the passenger travelling without a vehicle, and which entered civilian service during the six decades prior to *Caesarea*'s final crossing. Assembled, as nearly as possible, in chronological order are sections devoted to 53 ships, together with selected events from the sometimes colourful careers of a fleet which included some of the finest British-built vessels ever produced. This is primarily a collection of illustrations: they come from a number of sources, but in particular from the late Arthur Russell, a cross-Channel shipping expert and enthusiast, who would undoubtedly have approved of the use of his photographic collection in this way.

As an island with a dependence upon maritime links, Britain developed its cross-Channel routes very largely as a result of the enterprise of the railway companies, which attached great importance to the logical extension of their services across the sea. In 1939, the four main railway companies claimed ownership of no fewer than 164 vessels of a variety of types, and their fleets included ships of great beauty and technical innovation. Those employed in cross-Channel operations carried on a tradition which came to an end with the 1984 decision, based on the diminished significance of the rail-connected shipping services, that the railways should divest themselves of their marine interests.

It is my hope that this book will serve as a pleasant reminder to those who sailed in some of the ships depicted, or merely watched them, or an indication to those who wish they had, of the ships which once graced the waters around Britain and which now sail there no more.

John de S. Winser
Addington Hills, Croydon

An outline map of the routes regularly served by the ships featured in this book.

The Routes. Railway passenger ships sailed to Belgium and Holland from Harwich; to France from Dover, Folkestone, Newhaven, Southampton and Jersey; to the Channel Islands from both Southampton and Weymouth; to Ireland from Fishguard and Holyhead and to Northern Ireland from Lancashire and from the Scottish port of Stranraer. The routes on which the ships featured in this book regularly sailed are indicated on the accompanying map. Major railway passenger ships did not cover the Harwich–Antwerp route after World War II: the passenger service between Folkestone and Calais first opened in December 1946.

The motor vessel Cambria *which regularly served Ireland from Holyhead, between 1949 and 1975.*

The South Eastern Railway Company obtained steamship powers in the early 1860s. A SER paddle steamer is seen **above**, arriving at Folkestone and **below**, entering the port of Boulogne.

Prelude to 1920

Illustrated in this section, which leads up to the 1920 starting year of the book proper, are a few of the ships of the preceding decades.

Left: The 1890 Stranraer–Larne paddle steamer Princess Victoria arriving at her Scottish terminal.

The often heavy and cumbersome machinery of the paddle steamers gave way to more efficient twin-screw vessels. An example of this new generation of railway cross-Channel ships is Duke of Connaught, built in 1902 and pictured leaving Fleetwood.

The Queen, introduced in 1903 by the South Eastern & Chatham Railway was the first to be built with turbine propulsion. She was followed on the Strait of Dover routes by four similar ships – Onward, Invicta, Victoria and Empress – one of which is shown here passing through the entrance to Boulogne Harbour on arrival from Folkestone.

A contemporary vessel operating from the Lancashire port of Heysham for the Midland Railway Company was the 1904 Londonderry.

Opposite page: These two illustrations depict the 1905 steamer Dieppe, *which ran between her name port and Newhaven for the London, Brighton & South Coast Railway. In the lower photograph the ship is seen on the grid for attention to the underwater part of her hull. The railway companies operated their own Marine Workshops. Indeed, not only were the repair facilities under their ownership but so also were many of the ports themselves, and Newhaven was one such example.*

The 1907 Victoria *at Boulogne, possibly after arrival on the scheduled service from Dover which opened in 1921. Her funnels are seen here painted in the all-black livery which was used immediately after World War I.* Victoria *was the first Dover passenger steamer to have the new Southern Railway buff, with black top, colouring applied in June 1924. On one March 1926 crossing, the ship encountered such rough seas that her rudder was carried away.*

The 1912 London & South Western Railway sisters Normannia and Hantonia were the first to be built with geared turbines. Apprehension was reported in engineering circles as to whether they would be capable of standing the strain of continuous service. These misgivings proved unjustified and not only had both ships steamed about half a million miles on attaining their planned 25-year lifespans, but Hantonia went on to serve a further $1\frac{1}{2}$ decades and is seen here in her 37th year of operation.

A 1913 addition to the railway fleet was the Newhaven–Dieppe steamer Paris depicted **below**, with Dieppe, alongside the quay at her French terminal, where horsedrawn carriages and a boat train await her passengers. Boat trains were the accepted form of surface transport at each end of most Channel crossings, with at least one designated boat train, some bearing such famous titles as the "Irish Mail" (Euston–Dublin via Holyhead) or "Golden Arrow" (Victoria–Paris via the Short Sea Routes).

Biarritz and Maid of Orleans

Maid of Orleans *in the early 1920s, with funnels painted all-black.*

Biarritz *in July 1935, dressed overall for the Spithead Naval Review. By this time, the funnels of both ships had been lengthened and large windows had replaced the open sides of their Promenade Decks.*

The rowed mooring boat attends Biarritz *as she approaches her berth in Folkestone Harbour.*

Already alongside the Folkestone quay is the Southern Railway cargo vessel Minster.

In place of the passengers she was designed to carry, *Biarritz* first entered service during World War I, carrying mines which she laid, with considerable effect, in the eastern Mediterranean. Her sister started life transporting up to 2,200 troops per trip between Southampton and France and, when the conflict ended, both ships were assigned to bring the servicemen home, using ports they were later to frequent commercially. It was on the Dover–Calais route that *Maid of Orleans* entered peacetime service. *Biarritz*, on the other hand, made a somewhat belated civilian appearance on the service between Folkestone and Boulogne, her reconditioning at Barrow taking nearly two years because of strikes.

	Biarritz	**Maid of Orleans**
Port of Registry:	London	London
First owners:	South Eastern & Chatham Railway	South Eastern & Chatham Railway
Builders:	Denny, Dumbarton	Denny, Dumbarton
Gross tonnage:	2,053	2,071
Maiden civilian voyage:	1921	1920
End of railway service:	Retained on government work after World War II	Sunk, 1944

Both ships had the honour of carrying some very distinguished passengers in their time. The British Royal Family crossed from Dover to Calais and back aboard *Biarritz* in May 1923 and King George V was a passenger once again, two years later. Meanwhile, the 'Maid' had her share of publicity in connection with the State Visits to Britain, firstly of the Royal Family of Roumania then, shortly afterwards, of the King and Queen of Italy. In 1943, *Maid of Orleans* carried Winston Churchill from Gareloch to the liner *Queen Mary*. She was then isolated in Loch Long, for security reasons, until it was known that the Prime Minister had reached Canada safely.

Due to be replaced in 1940 by the new *Invicta*, *Biarritz* was reprieved by the outbreak of World War II and all three steamers were fitted out as infantry assault ships for the Normandy landings in June 1944. *Maid of Orleans* was sunk whilst returning from the beaches later that month. Her sister did not re-enter post-war commercial service but was employed on government work until being laid up at Southampton in 1948 prior to her demolition at Dover two years later.

Passengers disembark at Folkestone.

Biarritz is seen at Southampton Docks in her 1944 camouflage, and with assault landing craft suspended from special davits. She first arrived at the Normandy beaches on D + 1 (7th June).

Lorina

Two views of Lorina *leaving Guernsey, in Southern Railway colours, the LSWR having been absorbed into the SR in 1923. Most unusually, she carried an uneven number of lifeboats, four on the port side and three on the starboard, as the pictures on these two pages clearly reveal.*

Shortly before the outbreak of World War I in 1914, the London & South Western Railway placed an order for a passenger ship in the expectation that the vessel would be delivered in time for summer service in 1915. Also, that it would be one of two or even three additions to its Southampton fleet. The priorities of war not only left her abandoned on the slipway for well over two

years but also eliminated the possibility of any sister ships. It was not until early 1919 that *Lorina* reached Southampton and even then she was fitted out only as a troopship, despite the war having ended. It was on the last day of March 1920 that she first sailed from her home port with commercial passengers, destined for the Channel Islands and, after disembarking 250

16

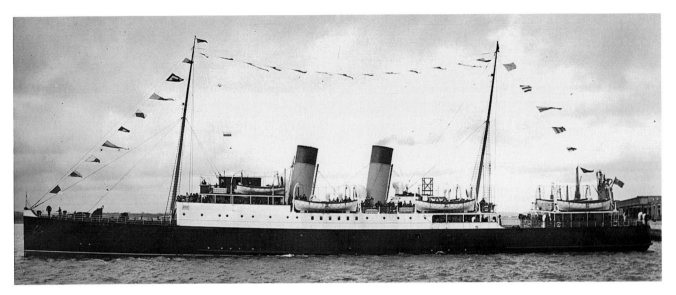

civilians in Jersey together with 200 naval and military personnel on leave, she was opened to the public so that local visitors could appreciate the latest deluxe unit of the LSWR fleet, later to be absorbed into the Southern Railway.

Like many railway ships, between scheduled sailings, *Lorina* occasionally ran excursions such as in 1936, from Cherbourg to Guernsey and Jersey and, in company with SR consorts *St Briac* and *Isle of Jersey*, to meet the Cunard White Star liner *Queen Mary* when she first called at Southampton for drydocking prior to her trials. March 1939 saw her on the Jersey–St Malo route; the following month she operated between Southampton and Havre and, in the summer months, served the Channel Islands from her home port. Early that September, she was sent to wartime Folkestone to cover the last remaining service to Boulogne but, on reaching the Kent port, notification was received that she had been requisitioned for government duty and was

The top picture shows Lorina *at Southampton in March 1936, on the occasion of the first arrival at the port of the liner* Queen Mary. *The bottom photograph may well have been taken on the same day. Part of her open deck had been plated in and her white paintwork increased since the photographs on the opposite page were taken.*

required at Avonmouth. Her career ended during the Dunkirk evacuation in the troopship role, in which it had begun 21 years earlier.

Port of Registry:	Southampton
First owners:	London & South Western Railway
Builders:	Denny, Dumbarton
Gross tonnage:	1,457
Maiden civilian voyage:	1920
End of railway service:	Sunk, 1940

Antwerp, Bruges and Malines

The Great Eastern Railway operated a popular cross-Channel service between Harwich and the Belgian port of Antwerp, and was anxious to resume full-scale passenger operations as soon as possible after the 1918 armistice. Accordingly, three new ships were introduced and all performed regular crossings. *Malines*, for instance, made an average of 97 round trips per year in her first 17 seasons on the Antwerp route. By that time part of the London & North Eastern Railway fleet, *Malines* became a floating hotel for five days in 1934, to accommodate 439 guests attending the Ipswich Agricultural Show. For this assignment she was moored in the river off Parkeston Quay and her guests were conveyed to and from the ship by motor boat. The following July, she embarked 280 passengers at Flushing for a cruise to the Naval Review at Spithead.

During World War II, *Bruges* was lost during the evacuation from Havre and her two sisters circumnavigated Africa in the role of Convoy Escort Vessels, their equipment including radar, Asdic and depth charge throwers. Neither returned to railway service afterwards, although *Antwerp* sailed from Harwich as a troopship and was, in 1950, considered by BR for conversion to a car ferry. This plan for *Antwerp* was not adopted nor was a post-war proposal that *Malines* should become a troop transport for the Harwich–Hook of Holland route.

This latter decision regarding *Malines* was taken as a result of the ship's poor condition caused by a torpedo attack at Port Said in 1942, which sank the vessel with a 36 ft hole in her starboard side, and buckled shell plating elsewhere. Raised and patched up, she nearly sank again in 1945 in heavy seas off the Portuguese coast when being towed home. Later that same year, while en route to the River Tyne, she was in more trouble when she broke adrift off the Isle of Wight and badly damaged the bows of a naval tug sent out from Portsmouth to assist her. She had also been no stranger to mishaps in her pre-war career, being involved in no fewer than six collisions in the 1920s and '30s. On one occasion the vessel which struck her sank and, on another, *Malines* herself went down by the stern in the shallows of the River Scheldt.

The steamer Antwerp *approaches her name port in July 1934.*

Bruges, *prominently displaying her LNER houseflag.*

The last of the trio to be completed for the Great Eastern Railway – Malines.

	Antwerp	**Bruges**	**Malines**
Port of Registry:	Harwich	Harwich	Harwich
First owners:	Great Eastern Railway	Great Eastern Railway	Great Eastern Railway
Builders:	John Brown, Clydebank	John Brown, Clydebank	Armstrong Whitworth, Tyne
Gross tonnage:	2,957	2,949	2,969
Maiden voyage:	1920	1920	1922
End of railway service:	Chartered out as peacetime troopship, 1945	Lost, 1940	Not repaired after war damage

Anglia, Hibernia, Cambria and Scotia

During the winter of 1919, the London & North Western Railway loaned its latest Holyhead passenger ship, *Curraghmore*, for the City of Dublin Steam Packet Company's Kingstown Mail service, while their usual steamers were undergoing overhaul. The following 28th November, the LNWR used *Curraghmore*, and the even newer *Anglia*, to perform the first sailings of the Irish Mail contract, which it had won on the strength of an ambitious order for four powerful sister ships, of which *Anglia* was the first. *Anglia* achieved a speed of over 25 knots on her trials, as did the second ship, *Hibernia*, which first reached Holyhead on that same November day. The keels of these two had been laid simultaneously in 1915 but progress was stopped so that resources could be devoted to naval production. Work was resumed in 1918, because the Royal Navy wanted their use as minelayers, but soon afterwards the war came to an end and with it the naval careers of HM ships *Anglesey* and *Sheppey*.

Delivery of the third vessel, *Cambria*, was affected by the general strike of shipyard joiners which started in December 1920. Because of this, her first visit to her home port of Holyhead was for coal while en route from her builder's yard to the French port of Rouen, which she reached on the last day of May 1921, so that French workers could progress her completion. She was back at Dumbarton at the end of October and made her maiden passenger voyage five weeks later, only to collide with a schooner en route and have to return to the Clyde for bow damage repairs. After the last ship had been delivered, the normal practice was to operate two of the steamers in continuous service for six weeks, to have the third vessel available on stand-by, while the fourth was laid off for overhaul. Poor financial results convinced the London, Midland & Scottish Railway, which had taken over in 1923, that economies were essential. *Anglia* was therefore laid up at Barrow and offered for sale. The lack of any acceptable offers in eleven years caused a little-used ship to be sent to the scrapyard, an unworthy end for one of a quartet which were described in LMS literature as the world's fastest merchant ships, bar two.

Although Red Ensign vessels, they were registered in

A splendid view of the Holyhead steamer Hibernia, *undergoing her trials.*

Cambria, as she appeared in her early days.

Eire, and it was thought that this was the reason why none of the remaining trio was immediately called up for government service in 1939. Registry was switched to London and *Scotia* was requisitioned and became a victim of enemy air attack at Dunkirk, her Captain and three members of his crew being decorated for their valour. *Cambria* and *Hibernia* remained on the Irish services throughout the war and had completed more than 28 years work by the time their replacements finally arrived.

This photograph of Hibernia was taken after a 1931 refit during which the forward end of her Promenade Deck was enclosed.

	Anglia	*Hibernia*	*Cambria*	*Scotia*
Initial Port of Registry:	Dublin	Dublin	Dublin	Dublin
First owners:	London & North Western Railway	London & North Western Railway	London & North Western Railway	London & North Western Railway
Builders:	Denny, Dumbarton	Denny, Dumbarton	Denny, Dumbarton	Denny, Dumbarton
Gross tonnage:	3,460	3,458	3,445	3,441
Maiden voyage:	1920	1920	1921	1922
End of railway service:	Sold for scrap, 1935	Sold for scrap, 1949	Sold for scrap, 1949	Sunk, 1940

Dinard and St Briac

Deck view, looking aft of the Southern Railway's St Briac.

Brittany was chosen as the main summer destination of these sisters. The fashionable holiday resort of Dinard faced the port of St Malo across the River Rance and initially, the service was a tidal one. This factor, on one occasion, trapped *Dinard* at the French terminal for over twelve hours when the rise in tide proved insufficient to float her at the advertised departure time.

Traffic on the Southampton cross-Channel routes proved disappointing in the early 1930s and, as an experiment, *St Briac* was diverted in 1932 to alternative employment. Six short cruises were offered and these were so popular that the vessel was annually utilised in this way, undertaking up to 24 cruises between Easter and late September, visiting a variety of ports mainly in the western Channel, although on occasion she did venture eastwards as far as Antwerp.

Although the cruising programme continued, *St Briac*

Dinard at Southampton's Berth 9 in the late 1930s.

Frequently used as a cruise ship, St Briac is seen here dressed overall during a call at Rouen.

was needed on her old route in the peak summer period. In 1938, traffic had increased by 77% compared with the previous year, so, for 1939, the spare Dover ship *Isle of Thanet* was transferred to perform an outward daylight sailing from Southampton each Thursday and Saturday, with a return crossing the following day. On 29th July that year, no fewer than three railway passenger ships departed for St Malo – *Dinard*, *Isle of Thanet* and the Jersey–St Malo steamer *Brittany*, between them carrying 1,878 passengers, with

St Briac performing the incoming sailing that night with 638 aboard.

Although never again was this Southampton–St Malo frequency repeated, *Dinard* did carry 630 vehicles during her one post-war season on the route, after her 1947 conversion into a car ferry. She had a career which did not end until nearly five decades of service had been completed, firstly under the British flag and finally under that of Finland, a tribute indeed to the quality of her construction.

St Briac alongside the quay of the Gare Maritime, at the Breton port of St Malo. On the move, in the background, is the railway steamer Brittany.

	Dinard	**St Briac**
Port of Registry:	Southampton	Southampton
First owners:	Southern Railway	Southern Railway
Builders:	Denny, Dumbarton	Denny, Dumbarton
Gross tonnage:	2,291	2,292
Maiden voyage:	1924	1924
End of railway service:	Sold for Baltic service, 1959	Sunk, 1942

St Julien and St Helier

These vessels, designed for the Great Western Railway's Weymouth–Channel Islands service, were built with two prominent funnels. The aft funnel, a dummy, was removed in 1928, firstly from St Helier, then from St Julien. The photographs **top opposite**, and **above**, give a good impression of St Helier, as built, while her sister is shown **bottom opposite** approaching St Helier Harbour, Jersey, as both steamers looked in the late 1930s. The darkness of the lower section of the funnels in these three photographs is indicative of the fact that GWR ships wore a distinctive red funnel colouring, with black top. They were the only railway-owned cross-Channel passenger steamers not to adopt the buff or yellow, with black top, scheme after the 'Big Four' railway companies were formed in 1923. These ships did eventually conform during the final stages of their 35-year careers, as can be seen from the illustration, **centre right**, of St Julien.

	St Julien	*St Helier*
Initial Port of Registry:	London	London
First owners:	Great Western Railway	Great Western Railway
Builders:	John Brown, Clydebank	John Brown, Clydebank
Gross tonnage:	1,885	1,885
Maiden voyage:	1925	1925
End of railway service:	Sold for scrap, 1961	Sold for scrap, 1960

Isle of Thanet and Maid of Kent

A House of Lords report in May 1923 drew attention to the fact that the cross-Channel steamers were carrying many more people on fewer Strait of Dover services than in pre-World War I days. Overcrowding and complaints were mounting to such an extent that the Southern Railway took the decision, in October 1924, that a new passenger steamer was essential and Isle of Thanet was launched at Dumbarton the following 23rd April.

Maid of Kent arriving at Folkestone in March 1939. Her final call at the port from Boulogne was on 2nd September that year, following which she was requisitioned for service as a Hospital Carrier: sadly she was destroyed by bombs at Dieppe the following May.

	Isle of Thanet	**Maid of Kent**
Port of Registry:	London	London
First owners:	Southern Railway	Southern Railway
Builders:	Denny, Dumbarton	Denny, Dumbarton
Gross tonnage:	2,664	2,657
Maiden voyage:	1925	1925
End of railway service:	Sold for scrap, 1964	Lost, 1940

Two views of Isle of Thanet, *which normally served the Strait of Dover routes. However, she is seen,* **right**, *during summer peak weekend duty on the Southampton–Guernsey route which she undertook in 1949, and from 1952 to 1958, when she would be one of six railway passenger ships sailing from Southampton within a few hours – four destined for the Channel Islands and one each for Le Havre and St Malo.*

The LMS Heysham–Belfast steamer Duke of Argyll.

Duke of Lancaster, Duke of Argyll, Duke of Rothesay and Duke of York

It is interesting to compare the appearance of Duke of York *in this photograph, as she was completed, with the later views of the vessel on page 30.*

Duke of Lancaster *in October 1944, during her service as a Hospital Carrier.*

The LMS Railway decided early in 1926 that three new ships should be ordered for their Belfast service, having already resolved that their routes from Fleetwood and Heysham should be amalgamated. Because of its potential for expansion, the latter port was subsequently chosen.

Officials and VIP guests on *Duke of Lancaster's* inaugural trip had an unexpected drama when the vessel was arriving back at Heysham. Following an entanglement with a dredger, the ship ended up stranded on a sandbank for over eight hours while her passengers were brought ashore by tender. This was but one of a series of mishaps which befell her during her first decade, the most serious of which was thought to have been caused by a careless smoker in 1931. The ship caught fire and sank alongside the quay at Heysham, an accident which put her out of service for over six months.

Duke of Rothesay was the 100th turbine vessel built by Denny, at its Dumbarton yard, situated at the confluence of the rivers Leven and Clyde. This remarkable firm, which constructed more than half of the ships featured in this book, had pioneered turbine propulsion for merchant vessels with the Clyde steamer *King Edward*, at that time only about half way through her impressive 50-year career.

In 1934 the LMS purchased for £75, a small launch which was lying at Poole and shortly afterwards sold it for scrap. The object of this action was to obtain use of the name *Duke of York* for a fourth new ship, such was the growing popularity of the route. Fitted out, not only with accommodation for 1,500 passengers, but also with space for mail, cars, general cargo and 316 head of cattle, *Duke of York* reduced the crossing time to under seven hours, within days of entering service.

As part of their early wartime commitments, both 'Argyll' and 'York' were sent to assist the 1940 evacuation from Guernsey, the latter vessel having previously come under fire at St Valery-en-Caux, where she was hit by a shell which failed to explode and was promptly thrown overboard by her Chief Officer. All four steamers were together during the early days of the Normandy invasion in June 1944. Only 'Lancaster' was initially intended to be a Hospital Carrier but 'Rothesay' was similarly converted, after an accident made her unsuitable for service as an assault ship. 'York', carrying six landing craft, sailed as *HMS Duke of Wellington*: 'Argyll', having served as a landing ship on D-Day, returning to the beaches that August as *Hospital Carrier No. 65*.

All survived initially to be restored to their pre-war route. However, following the loss of *Prague* from the Hook of Holland service, *Duke of York* was transferred to Harwich in 1948 and, after summer sailings from Southampton two years later, underwent a major refit which included the replacement of her original two funnels by one large one. In 1953 a serious collision in the North Sea necessitated the fitting of a new bow section, once again altering her appearance, as is apparent from the accompanying illustrations.

Duke of ...	Lancaster	Argyll	Rothesay	York
Port of Registry:	Lancaster	Lancaster	Lancaster	Lancaster
First owners:	London, Midland & Scottish Railway	London, Midland & Scottish Railway	London, Midland & Scottish Railway	London, Midland & Scottish Railway
Builders:	Denny, Dumbarton	Denny, Dumbarton	Denny, Dumbarton	Harland & Wolff, Belfast
Gross tonnage:	3,608	3,604	3,606	3,743
Maiden voyage:	1928	1928	1928	1935
End of railway service:	Sold for scrap, 1956	Sold for scrap, 1957	Sold for scrap, 1957	Sold for Mediterranean cruising, 1963

Duke of York *with a single funnel after her 1950/51 refit* **top** *and* **below**, *with a new raked stem following rebuilding necessitated by her 1953 collision.*
(Another photograph showing three of the 'Duke' vessels appears on pages 42/43.)

Worthing and Brighton

Above: *The Southern Railway's Worthing at Newhaven prior to 1932.*

The 1933 Brighton entering Newhaven Harbour.

Brighton *is seen here at her French terminal of Dieppe.*

Indicative of the predominently French ownership of the Newhaven–Dieppe fleet was the Southern Railway's choice of a Vicomtesse to perform the launching ceremony in 1928 of *Worthing*, the first of these two Red Ensign steamers. The decision that she should be oil-fired made it possible for her designers to allocate noticeably greater space to passenger accommodation than in her coal-burning predecessors on the route.

The London–Paris mileage was shortest via the Newhaven–Dieppe route, but the 64-mile sea sector, compared with the 21–26 miles of the Dover and Folkestone routes, made it competitively desirable for the Newhaven ships to be capable of higher speeds than any of the others on the Railway's English Channel routes. On her trials, *Worthing* completed the crossing in slightly over $2\frac{1}{2}$ hours, which is an interesting contrast to the advertised port-to-port time of four hours in the car ferry schedules sixty years later! *Brighton*, which was added to the fleet five years after *Worthing*, to become the fifth on the route to be so named, was required to maintain 24 knots in all weathers, compared with a norm of about 22 knots on the Strait of Dover railway services, and of under 20 on the Southampton routes.

Brighton was bombed in 1940 in one of the enclosed basins at Dieppe, after becoming trapped by the laying of magnetic mines. *Worthing* survived both the war and a serious collision with *HMS Hilary* in 1944 and the SR's early post-war plans envisaged her operating a daytime summer-only schedule on the Dieppe route and, if a bow rudder could be fitted, acting as a winter stand-by ship for the Strait of Dover services. This proposal was however overtaken by the 1947 restrictions on travel to the Continent as a result of which she was seriously considered for transfer to the Irish services that Christmas and the following summer. In fact, *Worthing* operated only one short spell from Folkestone and otherwise remained almost exclusively a Newhaven vessel, until her sale for work, firstly in the eastern Mediterranean, and later in the Red Sea.

Opposite, top, Worthing *is alongside the quay in* Dieppe, *while* Brighton *is in mid-harbour at buoys.*

Opposite, *A post-war view of* Worthing *at speed in the Channel.*
(Another photograph showing Brighton *appears on pages 2/3.)*

	Worthing	*Brighton*
Port of Registry:	Newhaven	Newhaven
First owners:	Southern Railway	Southern Railway
Builders:	Denny, Dumbarton	Denny, Dumbarton
Gross tonnage:	2,288	2,391
Maiden voyage:	1928	1933
End of railway service:	Sold to Greece, 1955	Lost, 1940

Canterbury

In its endeavour to improve the standards of cross-Channel service, the Southern Railway decided in January 1928 to introduce a new 1st class London–Paris $6\frac{1}{2}$-hour connection, to be called the "Golden Arrow", and to build a special ship for the Dover–Calais sea portion of this. This steamer was equipped with superior accommodation which included a Verandah Café, or garden lounge, an Observation Lounge and a Dining Saloon seating 100. She was certificated for 1,700 passengers but, in her "Golden Arrow" role, was expected to carry only 250–300. Despite this, she did have some 2nd class facilities including a Ladies' Saloon, a small restaurant seating 16 and a Gentlemen's Saloon with 23 sleeping berths.

As the new ship was being fitted out, in the shadow of Dumbarton Rock, the Channel Tunnel controversy, to continue spasmodically for many years after *Canterbury* had completed a lifetime of service, was already in progress. Prime Minister Baldwin announced in the House of Commons early in 1929 that, in view of the wide public interest in the project, the government was to re-examine the question. Enthusiasts appended to a Belgian cross-Channel steamer, stranded in Dover Harbour about that time, a banner bearing the inscription 'Why not a Channel Tunnel?'

Delivery of the new steamer was taken in Southamp-ton's No. 5 Drydock and the service was started on 15th May 1929, with non-premium and 2nd class passengers travelling shortly afterwards aboard a separate steamer, which that day was *Maid of Kent*. This duplication in sailings did not result in the desired boost to traffic and, two years later, the sailings were combined. Nevertheless the "Golden Arrow" service remained a feature of international surface travel for each peacetime year for over a quarter of a century after *Canterbury* had been replaced in 1946.

Despite being displaced at Dover, *Canterbury* still served Calais frequently on a new post-war service from Folkestone and also regularly plied from that Kent port to Boulogne, often in her later years carrying passengers on day excursions. In this she was continuing a tradition going back several decades: in 1923, for instance, the steamer *Victoria* had made Folkestone the starting point for excursions to Dieppe, Boulogne, Calais and Ostend. The cross-Channel scene was deprived of a much loved friend, when, at the respectable age of 35, *Canterbury* was finally withdrawn from service.

Designed originally for the SR's "Golden Arrow" service, Canterbury *is seen here in three views off Folkestone, post-World War II.*

Port of Registry:	London	Gross tonnage:	2,912
First owners:	Southern Railway	Maiden voyage:	1929
Builders:	Denny, Dumbarton	End of railway service:	Sold for scrap, 1965

Vienna, Prague and Amsterdam

	Vienna	*Prague*	*Amsterdam*
Port of Registry:	Harwich	Harwich	Harwich
First owners:	London & North Eastern Railway	London & North Eastern Railway	London & North Eastern Railway
Builders:	John Brown, Clydebank	John Brown, Clydebank	John Brown, Clydebank
Gross tonnage:	4,218	4,220	4,220
Maiden voyage:	1929	1930	1930
End of railway service:	Sold for government service, 1941	Sold for scrap, 1948	Sunk, 1944

Early in 1928, the London & North Eastern Railway, having invited ten shipyards to tender, accepted a quotation from John Brown of Clydebank for a new steamer for its Harwich–Hook of Holland route, with sleeping accommodation for 400 1st class and 100 2nd class passengers. The LNER agreed to make a bonus payment if the ship was delivered by the following 14th July, and to receive compensation if the vessel was late.

As building of this ship progressed on schedule, traffic from Harwich was so good that the specification was changed to enable a further 50 1st class berths to be installed and two more vessels were ordered. The final naming selection was reduced to four: *Locarno* was

The LNER's Prague *alongside at Hook of Holland in July 1934.*

not adopted but the cities of Vienna, Prague and Amsterdam were decided upon for the names of this trio. It was to be another 17 years before any larger ship was introduced into railway service.

In 1932, *Vienna* became a cruise ship at summer weekends, an experiment which proved sufficiently profitable for the company to be able to up-grade the ship's passenger facilities four years later by extending the Boat Deck and providing a 40-seat Cocktail Lounge. This perhaps explains why an inclusive charge of £10 10s was made to *Vienna*'s passengers, but only

Preparing for the restoration of the post-war Hook of Holland passenger service, two views of Prague *at Parkeston Quay, Harwich, in November 1945.*

£9 9s to *Amsterdam*'s when both ships cruised from Harwich to the 1937 Coronation Naval Review at Spithead, with a combined total of 530 passengers.

Prague did sterling work during the Dunkirk evacuation in June 1940 but only narrowly survived: she was so badly damaged that she did not steam again until December 1941. That same year, *Vienna* was acquired by the government and ended her days as a post-war cross-Channel troopship. *Amsterdam* carried American servicemen to the notorious Omaha beachhead on D-Day in 1944 and, following conversion for hospital ship duty, was mined off the French coast.

After an austerity reconditioning at Southampton, *Prague* was able to return to her pre-war route in November 1945, making six crossings each week. She was later sent to her builders for full refit, the work to include the installation of an automatic sprinkler fire-fighting system. Unfortunately, this precaution proved too late: she was engulfed by flames for two-thirds of her length whilst at Clydebank in March 1948. The vessel settled on the mud, practically full of water and, when subsequently refloated, was found to be too badly damaged for further service.

Left, The Southern Railway's Channel Islands steamer, Isle of Jersey, *as built.*

The first two of this trio were introduced on the Southern Railway Southampton–Channel Islands service in 1930 and, because of the increased traffic, *Isle of Sark* followed two years later. The latter was distinguishable from her earlier half-sisters not only because of her shorter masts and funnels, but also by her modified Maierform hull design, intended to increase stability and reduce fuel consumption.

In March 1936, *Isle of Sark* became the first ship in the world to be equipped with fin stabilisers and, on a rough crossing the following month, it was noted that they had reduced a 10-degree roll by half. A demonstration cruise was subsequently arranged during which the device was put into reverse, and the ship started to roll appreciably, despite the smooth water all round.

All three ships survived their various wartime tasks and *Isle of Guernsey* reopened civilian cross-Channel

Below, Isle of Sark *at Jersey in pre-war days; her graceful lines are shown up here to good advantage.*

Isle of Jersey, Isle of Guernsey and Isle of Sark

Isle of ...	Jersey	Guernsey	Sark
Port of Registry:	Southampton	Southampton	Southampton
First owners:	Southern Railway	Southern Railway	Southern Railway
Builders:	Denny, Dumbarton	Denny, Dumbarton	Denny, Dumbarton
Gross tonnage:	2,143	2,143	2,211
Maiden voyage:	1930	1930	1932
End of railway service:	Sold to Libya, 1960	Sold for scrap, 1961	Sold for scrap, 1961

The naval radar equipment fitted to HMS Isle of Sark is clearly visible in this December 1945 view, almost certainly taken at Portsmouth.

services when she left Newhaven at 09.17 on 15th January 1945, to reach Dieppe $4\frac{1}{2}$ hours later. *Isle of Sark* was exclusively fitted with surface warning radar for training purposes and therefore could not be spared by the Royal Navy until after the war in the Pacific had ended.

By Summer 1947, all three ships were together again, serving Jersey via Guernsey, sailing outwards overnight and returning by day. This schedule required a three-ship operation, as one vessel laid over in Jersey for 23 hours in order to ensure, for navigational safety

reasons, that arrival and departure was during daylight hours. An inward overnight service was actively considered by the SR but never adopted regularly.

The Southampton–Jersey journey time was $9\frac{1}{2}$ hours, except on one gale-swept occasion, when *Isle of Jersey* took no less than 62 hours to complete the voyage, after being forced to shelter firstly in the Solent, then in the Cherbourg Roads, and finally at Guernsey. During another rough crossing, three passengers were swept overboard and lost when a huge wave struck the ship.

At the very moment World War II started, Isle of Jersey, *already fitted out as a Naval Hospital Carrier, was entering the fleet anchorage at Scapa Flow. She is pictured here later in her wartime career.*

Performing one of the first commercial cross-Channel crossings for 4½ years, Isle of Guernsey is seen here leaving Newhaven for Dieppe in January 1945, four months before World War II ended.

*Still looking trim, despite 18 years' service in peace and war, Isle of Guernsey, **below**, in February 1948.*

(Another photograph of Isle of Jersey appears on pages 78/79.)

St Patrick

Port of Registry: London
First owners: Fishguard & Rosslare
                 Railways & Harbours
Builders: Alexander Stephen,
                 Glasgow
Gross tonnage: 1,922
Maiden voyage: 1930
End of railway service: Sunk, 1941

St Patrick *leaving Jersey. This ship was specifically intended to be a stand-by vessel for both of the Great Western Railway's major cross-Channel services, namely those from Weymouth to the Channel Islands and across St George's Channel between Fishguard and Rosslare. A 1930 report describes a plan to equip the vessel with portable cabins on the promenade deck which would be put to use when the steamer was on the Irish route, but removed each summer and the space utilised for tea lounges, when the steamer was operating the daylight Channel Isles sailings.*

In front of the attractive backdrop of St Peter Port, St Patrick *manoeuvres in Guernsey harbour.*

Princess Margaret and Princess Maud

	Princess Margaret	*Princess Maud*
Port of Registry:	Stranraer	Stranraer
First owners:	London, Midland & Scottish Railway	London, Midland & Scottish Railway
Builders:	Denny, Dumbarton	Denny, Dumbarton
Gross tonnage:	2,523	2,886
Maiden voyage:	1931	1934
End of railway service:	Sold to Hong Kong owners, 1962	Sold to Cypriot operators, 1965

Left, Both the LMS 'Princess' steamers served for three decades in railway service then went on to second careers elsewhere: Princess Maud *is depicted in her early days.*

Passenger traffic between Scotland and Ireland was strongly sought after by Burns & Laird, which operated directly from Glasgow to Belfast, and by the LMS Railway which provided a steamer link between Stranraer in Loch Ryan and Larne, with railway connections at each end. This competitive challenge prompted an LMS order for a new ship, the name of which used the route's traditional 'Princess' prefix to celebrate the Scottish-born sister of the present Queen.

In the early 1930s, shipbuilding prices were falling so that, when an improved version of *Princess Margaret* was delivered, the cost was about 10% less than the amount paid for her predecessor. This second vessel, which revived the name *Princess Maud*, first borne by a Stranraer vessel in 1904, proved to be the last conventional steamer built for this route. As a pioneering venture, the next ship constructed was the 1939 motor vessel *Princess Victoria*; the first stern-loading car ferry ever designed for cross-Channel service (see page 72).

Princess Maud was extensively involved in the 1940 evacuations from France. She transported 1,270 French soldiers from Dunkirk to the safety of Folkestone; rescued 1,000 servicemen from Veules des Roses, then carried 2,500 troops on one of the final crossings from St Malo. This Breton port, together with Guernsey, became regular destinations for the ship during the summer of 1951, while she was temporarily transferred to Southampton. Although her usual post-war railway employment was as a Holyhead-based vessel, she was not totally divorced from her old service: she was lent to other Irish routes when necessary and regularly sailed from Stranraer as replacement when *Princess Margaret* was away for annual overhaul.

Below: The scene at Heysham on 4th August 1939, with Princess Margaret, *temporarily transferred from Stranraer, nearest the camera. Astern of her are (right to left),* Duke of Lancaster, Duke of York *and* Duke of Rothesay, *all waiting to serve the busy route to Belfast. (Another view of* Princess Margaret *appears on page 77.)*

St Andrew and St David

	St Andrew	*St David*
Port of Registry:	London	London
First owners:	Fishguard & Rosslare Railways & Harbours	Fishguard & Rosslare Railways & Harbours
Builders:	Cammell Laird, Birkenhead	Cammell Laird, Birkenhead
Gross tonnage:	2,702	2,702
Maiden voyage:	1932	1932
End of railway service:	Sold for scrap, 1967	Sunk, 1944

Left: *Seen in this view undergoing her trials in March 1932 is St Andrew. In common with all other vessels on the Fishguard–Rosslare route, these two sisters were owned by the joint Irish and Great Western Railway company which was established when the passenger service opened. They were built to replace two of the original four ships which had started the service in 1906 and they perpetuated the names of two of them.*

Bottom opposite: St David, *probably setting out from the Mersey on her delivery voyage to Fishguard in 1932, and,* **below,** *the same vessel during her war service as a Hospital Carrier seen, in this 1942 photograph, at anchor off Inveraray, near the head of Loch Fyne, 90 miles from the open sea. The following June, in preparation for Mediterranean service, she was equipped with landing craft fitted out as water ambulances. Both ships assisted with casualties at the 1943 Sicily landings and went on to serve at the Anzio beachhead, where St David was sunk by attacking bombers. Her sister steamed 46,000 miles in the Mediterranean and carried over 15,000 patients before returning home, eventually to restore the passenger link between Wales and Ireland, for which she had been designed.*

Brittany

A railway steamer service had been operated between Jersey and France for 60 years when it was closed in 1914. Pressed by the Jersey authorities to open it again, the Southern Railway decided to do so in 1932, using an old ship, and ordered this new steamer to take over the following year. This decision, based on the tourist potential on the Jersey–St Malo route, proved a rather dubious one commercially and, as early as 1936, there were suggestions that, as an economy measure, the new *Brittany* should be offered for sale.

Scheduled sailings between Jersey and St Malo were seldom more than twice weekly, so *Brittany* was extensively employed on summer excursions between the Channel Islands themselves and to France, and became a Jersey-based ship for the season, refuelling from the Southampton 'Isle' mailboats, when necessary.

The ship steamed more than 10,000 miles in her first full year and her programme occasionally included charter sailings, such as from Guernsey to Cherbourg in 1936, when she took 600 passengers to see the liner *Queen Mary* make her maiden call at the port. Some years afterwards, *Brittany* worked with the QM's later consort when, dwarfed in Southampton's Ocean Dock, she embarked 160 French passengers who had arrived from New York aboard *Queen Elizabeth*.

When planning their post-war services, the SR contemplated the re-introduction of a Southampton–Caen service, last run in the early 1930s, and for this, *Brittany* would have been equipped with additional cabins. The

The Southern Railway Jersey–St Malo steamer Brittany *in pre-war days leaving Southampton.*

Brittany alongside the quay at St Malo.

route was expected to have passenger attraction because of the extent to which that part of Normandy had featured in the liberation of France. In this context, it was appropriate that the steamer had herself participated in the events of June 1944, having, as a Royal Navy auxiliary netlayer, set out moorings for Liberty ships supplying the allied forces. In 1945, *HMS Brittany* was being prepared for sailing to join the East Indies Fleet and would have done so, had the Pacific conflict not suddenly ended.

In the event, *Brittany* resumed a pattern of post-war sailings somewhat similar to her pre-1940 schedule. She completed her railway career in 1962 only to start another under a foreign flag. During her 39 years she made calls at more than 60 ports in 30 countries around the world, from Cape Town in the south, to Bombay in the east (both of these on war duty), and finally to the Baltic in the north – an achievement of quite exceptional variety.

Port of Registry:	Southampton
First owners:	Southern Railway
Builders:	Denny, Dumbarton
Gross tonnage:	1,445
Maiden voyage:	1933
End of railway service:	Sold to Finland, 1963

Brittany shows off her trim lines to good advantage in this view.
(Other photographs of this ship appear on pages 1 and 23)

Invicta

By the time *Invicta* was delivered in July 1940, northern France had been occupied by German forces and no employment was available for her. Whilst at her Gareloch mooring, she was considered for possible civilian use on the Irish cross-Channel services from Stranraer or Holyhead but was, instead, commissioned by the Royal Navy as an assault landing ship. It was in this capacity that, in the Dieppe raid in 1942, she made her first English Channel crossing, somewhat in contrast to the "Golden Arrow" service for which she had been designed as a further improvement in standards for Dover–Calais passengers. She eventually took up this peacetime assignment $6\frac{1}{2}$ years later than planned, having first been converted from coal to oil burning so that she could, if needed, be used on the Southampton–St Malo route during the peak summer season. In fact, she never strayed that far from Dover.

Her role might well have been down-graded if the Southern Railway had adopted an ambitious plan which was under active consideration even before the war ended. In order to combat expected air competition, consideration was given to the design of two smaller vessels each capable of carrying a train load of about 300 passengers between Dover and Calais in 45 minutes — half an hour quicker than by *Invicta*. To achieve this, a designed speed of more than 40 knots would be required (compared with *Invicta*'s 22), with the propellers being positioned below the hull. One-class passenger accommodation would be provided, mainly in open lounges, with facilities being limited to snack bars rather than a restaurant. The accompanying diagram indicates the difference in size and outline between *Invicta* and the projected vessels.

The plan was not adopted because of the uncertainty of such ships being able to achieve fast crossings regularly, or even venture out, in some of the rough seas encountered in the Strait of Dover. Reliability took precedence over speed because the sea crossing was such a vital link in an elaborate chain of international railway connections. This project was, however, yet another example of the forward thinking of the Southern Railway: it was not until SeaCat in 1991, 46 years later, that a record-breaking crossing time of under 45 minutes was officially achieved by a sea vessel, as opposed to a Hovercraft.

The projected high speed steamer, compared in size with Invicta.

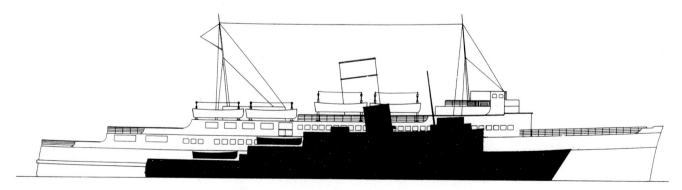

Opposite: Invicta *off Cowes, Isle of Wight, during her war service as an Infantry Landing Ship.*

Port of Registry:	London
First owners:	Southern Railway
Builders:	Denny, Dumbarton
Gross tonnage:	4,178
Maiden civilian voyage:	1946
End of railway service:	Sold for scrap, 1972

Invicta *reversing into Dover Harbour during her first season in commercial service on the SR's "Golden Arrow" route.*

Leaving Dover for Calais, Invicta *seen here about 1949. (Other photographs of* Invicta *appear on pages 5 and 77.)*

Arnhem and Amsterdam

	Arnhem	*Amsterdam*
Port of Registry:	Harwich	Harwich
First owners:	London & North Eastern Railway	British Transport Commission
Builders:	John Brown, Clydebank	John Brown, Clydebank
Gross tonnage:	4,891	5,092
Maiden voyage:	1947	1950
End of railway service:	Sold for scrap, 1968	Sold for Mediterranean cruising, 1969

Above: John Brown of Clydebank had been building vessels for the Harwich services since Copenhagen in 1907. Here, Arnhem of the LNER fleet, is seen sailing down the Clyde from her builder's yard in April 1947, prior to delivery for the Hook of Holland route.

Note the rearrangement of the side windows of Arnhem's Promenade Deck after her 1954 refit.

Amsterdam *and* Arnhem *at Parkeston Quay, Harwich, in May 1961. By the time* Amsterdam *joined* Arnhem *on the night service in 1950, the four railway companies were into their third year of nationalisation.* Amsterdam *had 1st class sleeping accommodation for 321, in single and 2-berth cabins, and for a further 236 passengers in 2- and 4-berth 2nd class cabins. She was built to replace the burnt-out* Prague: *a sister ship was contemplated but no order was ever placed. (Another photograph of* Amsterdam *appears on page 80.)*

Falaise and Normannia

First approved by the Southern Railway in April 1940 as a replacement for *Lorina*, the intervention of the war resulted in *Falaise* largely taking over the role played by *St Briac*. *Falaise* was the first Southampton-based vessel to benefit from the advanced science and technology which enabled an additional passenger deck to be added to the design without increasing the ship's length or affecting her ability to enter harbours where the depth of water or dimensions are limited.

Because of the seasonal nature of the traffic on the holiday route to St Malo, *Falaise* was available in the spring and early summer to undertake short cruises to the nearby Channel ports, as *St Briac* had done in pre-war days. Her most frequent call was ancient Rouen, six hours steaming up the River Seine. Two of her passengers on a May 1951 cruise to St Malo and Jersey were the senior British diplomats Burgess and Maclean, who shocked the nation by defecting from the ship to Russia — a pre-planned arrangement and no reflection on the service aboard *Falaise*!

At the end of World War II, the Southern Railway had hoped to introduce a train ferry between Southampton and Havre or Cherbourg, primarily designed for through freight wagons and cargo, but which would also have space for cars and accommodation for passengers. This project had still not been cancelled in 1949, which, when combined with the dwindling popularity of the Havre service in the pre-war decade, and

the French preference for the Dieppe route, probably explains the clear indications that a planned half-sister to *Falaise* was originally intended to double frequency on the Southampton–St Malo route.

The choice of name for the new ship was not instantly decided. At first *Atalanta* was proposed, reviving an association with cross-Channel services going back to 1836; then *Duke of Normandy* but, as this name was reserved for the States of Jersey tug, *Normannia* was finally selected, recalling the 1912 steamer which had been lost in 1940. *Normannia*'s Southampton career was concerned mainly with the Havre route and her occasional sailings to St Malo were in fact performed from Jersey.

Before *Falaise* was even launched, the Southern Railway had identified the future need for a car ferry operation between Newhaven and Dieppe. It was another twenty years before such a service was introduced and, with the planned run-down of the Southampton routes, the ship chosen to inaugurate it was *Falaise*. Accordingly, in 1963/64, both she and *Normannia* (intended initially for Dover car ferry service) underwent major refits and then emerged disfigured but ready for the new tasks ahead.

The Southern Railway's Falaise *in June 1947. She was the first merchant ship in the world to be delivered with Denny-Brown anti-roll stabilisers.*

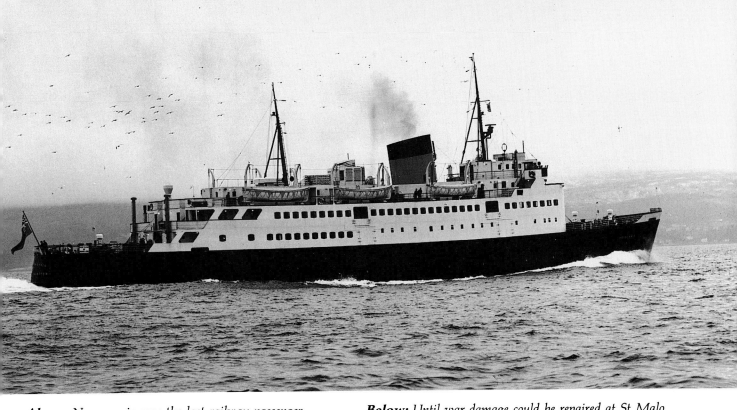

Above: Normannia *was the last railway passenger steamer built for the Southampton cross-Channel services. She is seen here undergoing her trials in the Firth of Clyde.*

Below: *Until war damage could be repaired at St Malo,* Falaise *anchored in the River Rance, and her passengers were carried between ship and shore by vedette.*

	Falaise	**Normannia**
Port of Registry:	Southampton	Southampton
First owners:	Southern Railway	British Transport Commission
Builders:	Denny, Dumbarton	Denny, Dumbarton
Gross tonnage:	3,710	3,543
Maiden voyage:	1947	1952
End of railway service:	Sold for scrap, 1974	Sold for scrap, 1978

Normannia *was one of eight railway ships which attended the Coronation Naval Review at Spithead in June 1953.*

Falaise, *during a cruise to the French Seine port of Rouen: one of 48 such calls during her career.*

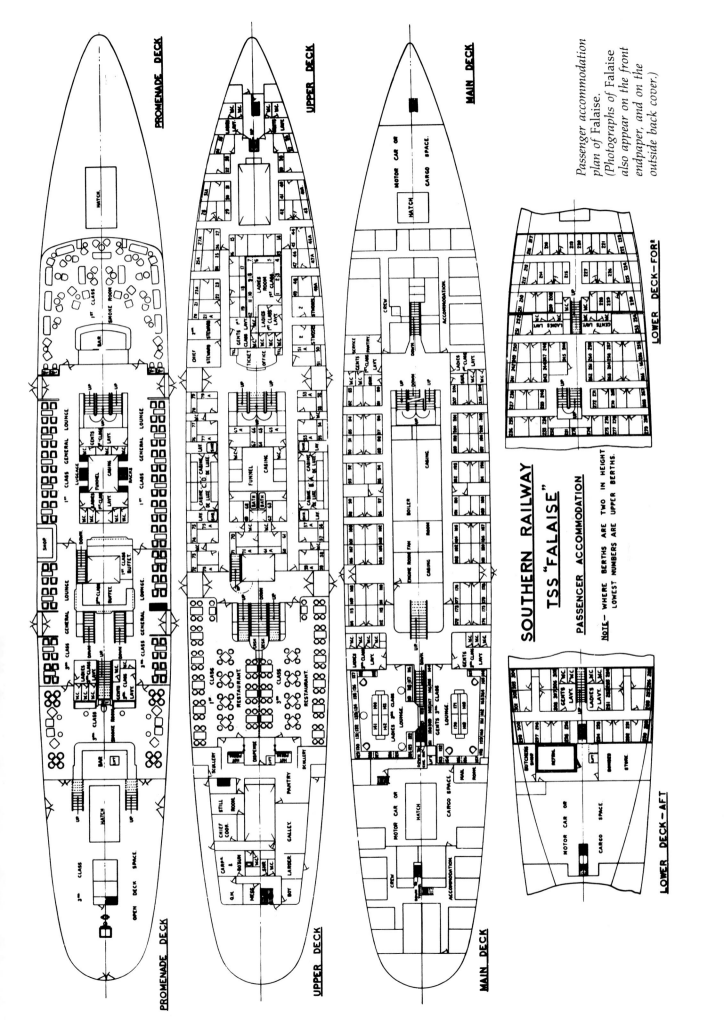

Passenger accommodation plan of Falaise. (Photographs of Falaise also appear on the front endpaper, and on the outside back cover.)

SOUTHERN RAILWAY

TSS "FALAISE"

PASSENGER ACCOMMODATION

NOTE— WHERE BERTHS ARE TWO IN HEIGHT LOWEST NUMBERS ARE UPPER BERTHS.

PROMENADE DECK

UPPER DECK

MAIN DECK

LOWER DECK—FORD

LOWER DECK—AFT

St David and St Patrick

	St David	**St Patrick**
Port of Registry:	London	London
First owners:	Fishguard & Rosslare Railways & Harbours	Fishguard & Rosslare Railways & Harbours
Builders:	Cammell Laird, Birkenhead	Cammell Laird, Birkenhead
Gross tonnage:	3,352	3,482
Maiden voyage:	1947	1948
End of railway service:	Sold for service in the eastern Mediterranean, 1971	Sold for service in the eastern Mediterranean, 1972

Two views of St Patrick, as she originally appeared. Her initial service was mostly from Fishguard and Weymouth: she later closed the Southampton railway passenger services to Havre and St Malo before being moved to the Strait of Dover. The lower photograph shows the vessel arriving at Jersey.

Apart from a brief initial spell on the Weymouth–Channel Islands service, St David *spent most of her days serving Rosslare from Fishguard, and just visible on her funnel in this August 1966 photograph are the letters FR, abbreviations for the joint British and Irish owning company.*

St Patrick *photographed in Weymouth Harbour. (Another view of* St Patrick *appears on page 4.)*

Hibernia
and
Cambria

M.V. "CAMBRIA" AND MAILBOATS IN HARBOUR, HOLYH

The motor vessel Cambria *at Holyhead* *with* Princess Maud *astern.*

Hibernia *begins another crossing.*

	Hibernia	*Cambria*
Port of Registry:	London	London
First owners:	British Transport Commission	British Transport Commission
Builders:	Harland & Wolff, Belfast	Harland & Wolff, Belfast
Gross tonnage:	4,972	4,972
Maiden voyage:	1949	1949
End of railway service:	Sold to Greece, 1976	Sold to Saudi Arabia, 1975

In British Rail colouring, Cambria *at sea.*

Hibernia *at Dun Laoghaire in January 1965.*
(Another photograph of Cambria *appears on pages 6/7.)*

By June 1939, tenders had been submitted to the LMS Railway for two new ships for the service between Holyhead and Kingstown (Dun Laoghaire). The contract went to Fairfields on the Clyde but, because of the outbreak of war, it was cancelled. The project was however revived in 1946, with the order this time going to Belfast, the first ship being due for delivery in March 1948 and the second three months later. Both vessels were to have stabilisers but their installation was later postponed as an economy measure.

When the ships finally appeared, about a year late, they were the first British cross-Channel railway pas-

senger ships to have diesel propulsion. They were also significantly larger than their Holyhead predecessors of the same name, having a total passenger capacity of 2,000 with sleeping accommodation for 436. Each ship devoted a lifetime to service across the Irish Sea and it was claimed that *Hibernia* had carried something in the region of 12 million passengers by the time she had completed her 27 years on the Holyhead route.

Maid of Orleans

The Southern Railway envisaged, as early as 1945, that car ferry facilities would one day be provided at the port of Folkestone. However it was 27 years before this became a reality. In the interim, reliance was placed on conventional ship designs and, in 1946, an order was approved for a new passenger steamer which spent most of her days operating out of Folkestone. In keeping with the revival of the name *Maid of Orleans*, a bronze equestrian statuette, representing Joan of Arc, was displayed in an illuminated alcove over the ship's main staircase.

The new vessel was another Dumbarton product and it was estimated that, in her first year of service, 70% of the two million Southern cross-Channel passengers travelled in Denny-built steamers. Although a 4,000-ton conventional passenger ship was due to be ordered for the Dover and Folkestone services in 1951, this ship never materialised and *Maid of Orleans* proved to be the last of her type to be acquired by the railways for their Strait of Dover routes. Thereafter all new ships were of the car ferry breed.

Port of Registry:	London
First owners:	British Transport Commission
Builders:	Denny, Dumbarton
Gross tonnage:	3,777
Maiden voyage:	1949
End of railway service:	Sold for scrap, 1975

Above: The Denny-built steamer Maid of Orleans.

Opposite top: In lively conditions, Maid of Orleans approaches Folkestone, stern first.

Right: A smoke deflecting funnel top was added to Maid of Orleans in 1959. (Another view of this ship appears on the rear endpaper.)

Left: Maid of Orleans sails out of Folkestone Harbour.

Top: Brighton *at speed.*
Below: *The vessel at Southampton in May 1950 prior to her maiden voyage. Alongside her is the railway owned Portsmouth–Ryde motor ship* Brading, *completed in 1948.*

Brighton

Three months after the outbreak of World War II, the Dover steamer *Invicta* was launched at Dumbarton and the Southern Railway reserved the vacated slipway for a replacement for their 1913 Newhaven–Dieppe steamer *Paris*. However, the French partners on the route already had three ships of their own under construction and understandably were not able to provide the major part of the funding for the building of yet another one. This plan was therefore shelved and not revived until 1947 but three years later, this new 24½-knot ship became a passenger-carrying reality.

Brighton proved to be the last British passenger steamer built for service between Newhaven and Dieppe, a route on which, as early as 1911, parliamentary powers had apparently been sought by the railways for the introduction of train ferries. This plan was killed off by the start of World War I three years later, but it was the introduction of the car ferries which affected *Brighton*'s career and caused her premature disposal from railway ownership.

Port of Registry:	Newhaven
First owners:	British Transport Commission
Builders:	Denny, Dumbarton
Gross tonnage:	2,875
Maiden voyage:	1950
End of railway service:	Sold for Jersey Lines service, 1966

Londres

The sale of the British Newhaven–Dieppe steamer *Worthing* in 1955 left *Brighton* as the sole remaining Red Ensign vessel on the route. To correct this imbalance, *Londres* was selected for the second change of nationality of her career. Still under construction when France was overrun by Germany in 1940, she served with the German Navy until 1945. Her first call at Newhaven took place in December of that year, on her way to being converted ready to commence peacetime passenger service in 1947 under the French flag. During the winter of 1954/55, she underwent a refit at Barry prior to starting her first commercial sailing under British registry, in which capacity she completed 1,528 crossings before being made redundant by the impending inauguration of car ferry services.

British Port of Registry: Newhaven
First owners: French Railways
Builders: Forges et Chantiers, Havre
Gross tonnage: 2,434
Maiden British voyage: 1955
End of railway service: 1963

Londres leaving Newhaven. She was equipped with an unusual type of davit which enabled the three after lifeboats on each side to be raised six feet above deck level, when sea conditions were favourable. With the boats raised, the deck area for passengers was greatly increased: in this view, one of the port lifeboats is so raised.

Duke of Lancaster, Duke of Argyll and Duke of Rothesay

It is said that, as early as 1895, Denny had earned the reputation of being the world's finest builders of light draft ships: by the time it closed in 1963, the firm had completed no fewer than 78 railway cross-Channel passenger, cargo and car ferry vessels for British waters. *Duke of Rothesay* was the third of a trio built to replace the 1928 Heysham steamers of the same name and the last of a distinguished line of railway passenger steamers completed at Denny's Dumbarton yard.

Duke of Lancaster was destined to have a railway career of considerable variety, being designed not only for the Northern Ireland link but also for international

Above and below: Duke of Lancaster: *her public rooms were claimed to be models of superb design and faultless taste.*

cruising. As such, she embarked her first passengers from Heysham and Dun Laoghaire in May 1958 and set sail for Southampton to undertake three 6-day cruises to Amsterdam, Ostend and Rouen. These were repeated the following year and, in addition, a 9-day September cruise was offered which took the ship into Scottish waters, amidst spectacular West Highland scenery and to the islands of Mull, Lewis, Skye and Iona.

Variations of the Scottish Lochs cruise were featured for the following seven seasons but these did not exclude her Continental cruises which became annually more ambitious. In 1960, she was in the West Jutland port of Esbjerg for two days; the following year she called at Bergen and cruised in the fjords while, in 1962, she took her 312 passengers to the Outer Hebrides, to

the Norwegian ports of Kristiansand and Oslo, on to Copenhagen, then home through the Kiel Canal.

In 1964 and in '65, *Duke of Lancaster* sailed southwards, from Southampton, Heysham and Plymouth, making calls at Corunna, Lisbon, Vigo and Western France. In 1966, she left Heysham at the end of April for France, Portugal and Spain, then, in mid-May, set out from Southampton for Dutch, Danish, Swedish and Norwegian ports. Four Scottish itineraries that season completed her cruising career.

It was inevitable that the ever-increasing need to cater for the motorist would affect the 'Dukes'. All three were converted for car ferry duty, *Duke of Rothesay* being assigned to Fishguard in 1967 and her two sister ships to start 1970 drive-on/drive-off operations on their old route to Belfast.

Duke of ...	Lancaster	Argyll	Rothesay
Port of Registry:	Lancaster	Lancaster	Lancaster
First owners:	British Transport Commission	British Transport Commission	British Transport Commission
Builders:	Harland & Wolff, Belfast	Harland & Wolff, Belfast	Denny, Dumbarton
Gross tonnage:	4,797	4,797	4,780
Maiden voyage:	1956	1956	1956
End of railway service:	Sold for static use at Llanerch-y-Mor, North Wales, 1979	Sold for Mediterranean service, 1975	Sold for scrap, 1975

Duke of Rothesay *was the last of the long line of railway cross-Channel passenger ships to be completed by Denny, Dumbarton.*

Left: The Channel Islands steamer Caesarea, as she started service, when her funnel colouring was buff and her hull black, and **opposite**, as she appeared later with a blue hull and the British Rail symbol on a red funnel.

Sarnia *was the last railway passenger steamer to be built for English Channel service.*

Caesarea and Sarnia

	Caesarea	**Sarnia**
Port of Registry:	Weymouth	Weymouth
First owners:	British Transport Commission	British Transport Commission
Builders:	J. Samuel White, Cowes	J. Samuel White, Cowes
Gross tonnage:	4,174	4,174
Maiden voyage:	1960	1961
End of railway service:	Sold for use in Hong Kong, 1980	Became a floating supermarket, 1978

Soon after the 1948 nationalisation of the four railway companies to form one British Railways organisation, consideration was given to replacing the two Weymouth ships, *St Julien* and *St Helier*, which were by then too small and very old fashioned. Before their successors actually appeared, another eleven years had elapsed, and they took over not only from the two 'Saints' but also from the three 'Isles', whose Channel Island route from Southampton was closed in favour of an amalgamated service on the 32-mile shorter route from Weymouth.

The new ships, named *Caesarea* (the Roman name for Jersey) and *Sarnia* (Guernsey), each had a passenger capacity of 1,400 which was identical to that of the 1930 *Isle of Jersey*, when built. However, *Caesarea*'s gross tonnage of 4,174 was nearly double that of the older vessel, a comparison which gives some indication of the additional space available for passenger amenities in the thirty years of development which the new design represented. Some idea of price escalation during that time can be judged from the fact that, at £1½

million, *Caesarea* was about nine times more expensive than *Isle of Jersey* and double the price of the 1952 *Normannia*.

Despite the impact of air travel, interest in the new ships can perhaps be gauged from the fact that *Caesarea* was inspected by 18,200 people when she made her first publicity visit to Jersey. A report, written after her 1971 refit, describes the attractive Andaman padavk and East Indian rosewood panelling of *Sarnia*'s 95-seat smokeroom and bar, at the forward end of her promenade deck. Mention is also made of her two luxury suites, each with private bathroom and shower, of the 118 adjustable reclining seats on her main deck amidships, and of the 20,000 sq ft of wood veneers used in her construction.

Together, the sisters served Guernsey and Jersey until, in 1976, as *Sarnia* prepared to hand over to the car ferries at Weymouth, *Caesarea* was moved to the Strait of Dover to operate five final years of railway ship sailings, designed exclusively for the non-motorist.

Opposite: Sarnia *in September 1975. (Other photographs of* Sarnia *appear on the outside front cover and on page 80.)*

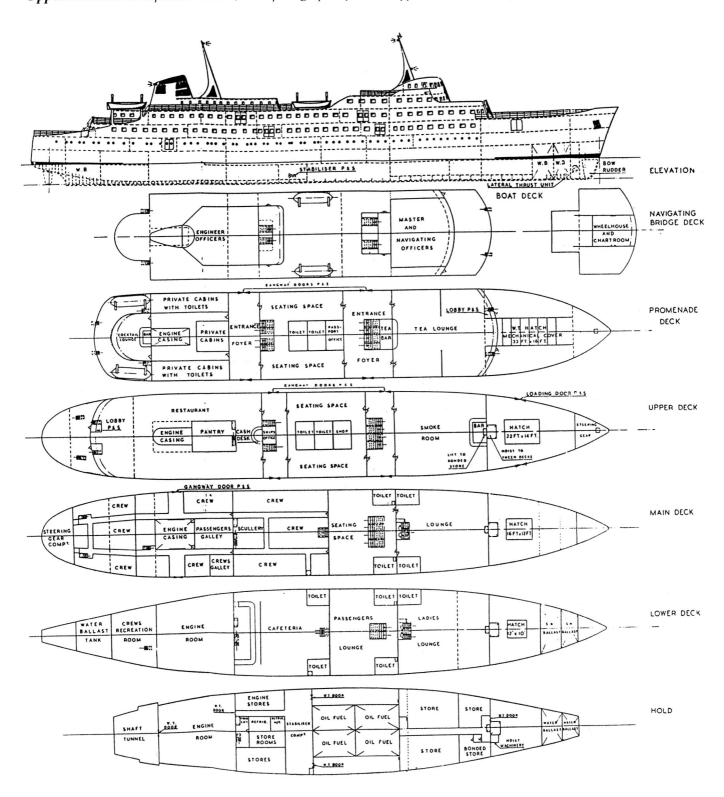

ELEVATION

BOAT DECK

NAVIGATING
BRIDGE DECK

PROMENADE
DECK

UPPER DECK

MAIN DECK

LOWER DECK

HOLD

In a 1955 report to a committee of the British Transport Commission, certain designs were recommended for future cross-Channel vessels. The proposal regarding passenger ships was undoubtedly a radical one inasmuch as it advocated the engines being placed aft and propulsion by twin-screws driven by gas turbines. The recommended design is shown above although, in the event, no such advanced design was ever adopted.

Avalon

Port of Registry:	Harwich
First owners:	British Railways Board
Builders:	Alexander Stephen, Glasgow
Gross tonnage:	6,584
Maiden voyage:	1963
End of railway service:	Sold for scrap, 1980

Opposite: Avalon, *approaching Harwich in 1963, makes a fine sight. Despite the recommended design detailed on page 69, Avalon was larger than, but not markedly dissimilar from, her predecessors on the Harwich–Hook of Holland route. She combined her cross-Channel sailings with international cruising, in which role she was limited to carrying only 350 passengers. She was photographed below in September 1972, entering Dover Harbour after completing a cruise to Gibraltar. Her cruising schedules included visits to more than 35 different European and North African ports with destinations as diverse as Leningrad and the Arctic Circle, in the north, and Agadir and Casablanca, in the south – places never before contemplated for railway ships in peacetime. After eleven years' service, all this came to an end and Avalon was sent for the seemingly inevitable conversion for car ferry operations. She carried with her the distinction of being not only the last but also the largest conventional, or 'classic', British cross-Channel railway passenger ship ever constructed.*

Other Contemporary British Railway Ships

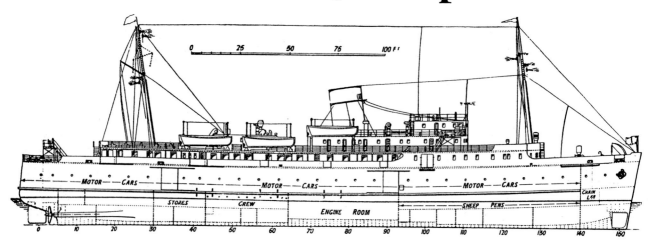

The Car Ferries

The first drive-on/drive-off car ferry service was pioneered in 1939 between Stranraer and Larne by the LMS Railway using the specially designed Princess Victoria *(illustrated* **top***). Two months after entering service, she was requisitioned for minelaying duties and, less than a year old, was sunk, ironically by a mine.*

The 1952 Lord Warden *— the first Strait of Dover railway ship to be especially designed for cars — is seen here on her trials.*

In 1959, Lord Warden *was joined on the Dover–Boulogne route by the popular* Maid of Kent, *also a stern-loading steamer. In this October 1981 picture she is seen at Weymouth.*

Vehicles could be handled on the motor vessel Senlac, *through both bow and stern doors. She took her name from the hill near Hastings where William the Conqueror won his famous victory in 1066.* Senlac *started service from Newhaven in 1973 and is photographed in this view entering her French terminal port of Dieppe in September 1983.*

The Cargo Ships

The railways operated a considerable fleet of vessels which were primarily for the carriage of cargo and/or cattle. This is the 1921 Holyhead cargo vessel Slieve Donard (**top**). Some of the cargo vessels had accommodation for passengers, most notably the 450-capacity Great Western, which served Waterford from Fishguard. She operated this route for much of World War II, early in 1945 being escorted by a destroyer and motor gunboat as protection against enemy submarine attack.

Left: Deal, one of nine similar ships introduced by the SR in the second half of the 1920s for its Western Channel and Strait of Dover cargo services.

Below: The motor vessel Winchester, built for the SR Southampton cargo routes in 1947.

The Train Ferries

Shepperton Ferry, *one of a trio of SR train ferry vessels built for the Dover–Dunkirk route. Her sister,* Twickenham Ferry, *was the first to be delivered in July 1934 but, problems connected with the construction of the special dock at Dover, to deal with a tidal variation of up to 25 feet, delayed the start of the service until October 1936. Shortly before this, bowing to political pressure from France,* Twickenham Ferry *was transferred to the French flag. On her publicity voyage, she damaged her stern on arrival at Dover, derailing one of the sleeping cars and doubtless not greatly pleasing some of her VIP guests who were obliged to transfer to another part of the train. The Dover–Dunkirk route, with its "Night Ferry" through Sleeping Car service between London and Paris and day crossings catering for freight and cars, started to become profitable in 1947.*

Suffolk Ferry, *seen here at her Continental terminal of Zeebrugge, operated on the cargo-only train ferry service to Harwich.*

37486. SOUTHERN RAILWAY STEAMER. "RYDE".

The Isle of Wight Ships

*Railway ships served the Isle of Wight from Lymington and Portsmouth. **Left**, is seen one of the passenger vessels which regularly connected the island with the mainland. She is the paddle steamer Ryde, introduced by the Southern Railway in 1937 and seen coming alongside Ryde Pierhead.*

The Clyde Steamers

***Below**, is an example of a one-time extensive railway fleet which served the population of the Firth of Clyde and its visitors. The motor vessel* Maid of Ashton *was the first of a quartet constructed for the Clyde service in 1953.*

MAID OF ASHTON

Miscellany

Princess Margaret *at Stranraer.*

The Dover–Calais steamer Invicta.

Photograph Credits

Very grateful thanks are extended to all those who kindly supplied the following photographs.

Aberdeen University	Page 8 (Centre)
Associated British Ports via Southampton City Museums	Pages 22 (Top & Bottom), 26(T), 31(T), 38(T), 46, 49(T)
John Clarkson	Page 27(B)
Alex Duncan	Pages 27(T), 60(B), 74(C), 77(B), 80(T)
FotoFlite, New Romney, Kent	Pages 1, 33(B), 34, 35(B), 49(B), 60(T), 62(T), 66(B), 74(B), 75(T), 78/79, Rear Endpaper

Phil Fricker — Front Endpaper, page 54(B)

Glasgow University Archives — Pages 42(T), 52, 53(T), 72(B), Outside Back Cover(T)

Ambrose Greenway Collection — Pages 21(T), 28(T)

F. W. Hawks Collection — Pages 13(B), 17(T), 18, 28(B), 36, 41(T), 58(C)

Lancaster City Museums — Pages 42(B)/43

Maritime Photo Library — Page 25(C)

F. R. Sherlock — Page 30(B)
Pat Sweeney — Page 74(T)
Wright & Logan — Page 39(T)

The other photographs were supplied by British Railways/Sealink or were selected from the author's own collection, or are from the camera or collection of Arthur Russell.

Isle of Jersey, *around 1947.*

The Harwich steamer Amsterdam *which joined her sister* Arnhem *on the Hook of Holland night service in June 1950.*

Sarnia, *leaving Weymouth in 1973.*